"I always wanted to be a dog
but I hesitated
for I thought they lacked certain skills.
Now I want to be a dog."

Michael Ondaatje

Poodles & Pix

A Poetry Collection

by

Xavier Jarrell McClinton

TAMALPAIS
PRESS

Print Edition ISBN 978-0-9906831 1-7
Library of Congress Control Number: 2022903098

First print edition April 2022.

Edited by Daniel Kunstler
Cover art by Xavier Jarrell McClinton and Daniel Kunstler
Photographs by Xavier Jarrell McClinton

Typeset in EB Garamond
Printed in the USA.

Tamalpais Press
Marin County
California

To my daughter Jazzaray.

For her I have strived to be the best father I can be.
She inspires me to shape the very best version of myself.

CONTENTS

I.   A Boo & His Spoo Crew   3

II.   Brother Winston   11

III.   Love   23

IV.   Inspiration   35

V.   Introspective   51

VI.   The Pandemic   71

VII.   Injustice   81

VIII.   Loss   87

IX.   Friendship   95

X.   Pain   103

XI.   The Struggle   115

XII.   Abstract   127

XIII.   Hope   135

I.

A Boo & His Spoo Crew

Meant To Be

The infatuation began as a child
Surrounded by machismo,
They thought the idea wild
The moment I witnessed their beauty, grace
I knew it was only a matter of time, space

My hood was sometimes kinda scary
With some dogs, got kinda hairy

When ever I mentioned a Poodle,
"They're too fofo", they'd profess
I'd whisper to myself,
"What dog is the smartest!"

On a journey some forty plus years later,
The dream is now a reality
And as long as I can manage,
It will only be Spoos for me.

What I did not know
Would contribute to further my thirst
The one never to be last,
because he came first

Just as the world was shook up
by Ali's knockout of Sonny Liston
So shook my heart the first moment
I laid eyes on Brother Winston

I don't know if you heard,
My IHMA Warrior, B-Dub,
Turned four on September third.

I didn't really know.
I know now.
How much they give
and take like family

Once just hopefully
Now I can see
B-Dub and me
We're meant to be

✳

If You Don't Mind

I came home during hard times
Illness, police brutality, hate crimes

From coast to coast my ass
Flew in first class
The trip wasn't short

I could tell his smell
It felt right
Upon first sight,
At the airport

Yup, I'm a pup,
What I feel is real
My Papi,
 I completely trust

Respect is earned
Not learned
Love isn't provisional
It's unconditional
I'm the filling,
Papi's my crust

We're two of a kind,
Time we can't rewind
So since we're aligned
I'll stay a while,
If you don't mind.

*

Zamora

I remember where I was,
The day it happen
Pumping some iron,
Listening to Snoop rapping'
Singing "slim with the tilted brim."
Soon after,
No more laughter
Things turned kinda grim

Zamora on my mind
In the background
With thoughts of a different kind
Would B-Dub even be around?
IMHA is what they found
Could life be this unkind?
Yes, and there is no rewind

Hoping for the best,
Preparing for the worst
Surly it's to early,
To lose my first
I was a hot mess
Others feeling unrest

Brother Winston was sleeping
Heart breaking,
I lay over him weeping
I began to whisper
I want you to know
That if you go,
I'll miss you so

Did all I could for ya
As your Papi
My life you've graced,
You'll never be replaced,
My heart will heal with Zamora

Now look at you,
You're pulling through,
Support and prayers,
From a few
For me thankfully,
 It's not either or
Grateful for the restart,
Room in my heart
To love one more

✳

II.

Brother Winston

In 2021 Winston was stricken with Immune-Mediated Hemolytic Anemia, or IMHA, an often fatal canine autoimmune disease whereby the dog's body attacks its own red blood cells. It took a village to save him. The village came through. Bless the village.

Good To Be Alive

Oh boy! It's good to be alive
Wasn't sure I was gonna survive
 I should mention something notably
This disease was not in my family tree

There are lots of good ones,
But I love my Papi
Nursing me back
So that I'm healthy

They call it physical therapy
Wherever I land,
He'll ensure I'm the best I can be

We'll enjoy whatever time
we have left with love
We fit together
like puzzle pieces
Hand in glove

The love we share is why I thrive.
Yesterday has passed.
Tomorrow isn't promised.
 So today it's good to be alive

✳

My White Light

A fluffy, cuddly, snuggly, ball of hair
From the first night he had that flare

To do his business,
He rang the bell
He learned quickly
Smart as hell

Shortly thereafter
He began to master,
Courses in agility
With all his ability,
He appreciated tranquility

Now a teenager.
The fact
He's intact
Made people ask:
Will he, or won't he

My little ranger,
At the park,
Before dark,
Gotta Willy Nilly
When he saw Miss Lily

Embraced the roll
With soul   ˙
As big brother
Irreplaceable.
You're like no other
You trusted our love,
Allowed us to have another

You give me more
Than I could've ever known
When you came through the door
I knew you were on loan

I hope time will take it's time
So we can enjoy each and everyday
The love that will never stray

We don't worry about the past
We live everyday as if it's our last

✴

Don't Wanna Be Right

Relationships are tough,
Don't always go well
In fact,
They are hard as hell
Think you know,
You can never tell
Uh oh, too late
You didn't gel

That's not us,
Plus you can trust,
I'll always fight
If loving you is wrong,
I don't wanna be right

Started looking,
It was you I found
You're not just mine,
You're world renowned

We know what we have
The love we share
I won't hide
Or how much I care
My heart has no reason

To feel contrite
So goes the song
If loving you is wrong,
I don't wanna be right

As long as you're here,
I will be there
I'll tell you what I fear
Early departure ain't fair

So we'll love
Each and everyday
Whatever happens,
Come what may

You are my lantern
My guiding light,
Shining so bright
If loving you is wrong,
I don't wanna be right

*

Say A Little Prayer

It may be cloudy outside,
My heart shines inside
Holding on by a thin rope
Tied to a pillar of hope

Life is just not fair,
Today there's less despair
Emotionally, we are there
Because you care
And said a little prayer

Couldn't see the forest through the trees
On my knees,
Begging please,
Looking to the sky.
Asking: why?

Been quite the scare,
I said a little prayer

Many roads lead to Rome
I'll take the one that brings him home

Under observation.
All we can do is wait
Allow the transfusions to help his blood
Regenerate.

We may survive this with time to spare
Thanks to UC Davis
A thong,

And a little prayer

*

Day By Day

There was a time
For a while,
He had no grin
Wondered if I'd ever see that smile,
On his face again

Face sinking in,
Hind legs thin
On the brink,
Of losing my best friend

Plenty of trees left, but I see the forest
I can hear the prayers,
Good vibes like a chorus

Ridding the bull of life ain't gonna throw us
What do you need
B-Dub? A kiss?
A belly rub?
You're a warrior.
You ain't no scrub.

I want to see you get strong, back to healthy.
While I want for you,
I can't forget quality time for me

As long as you have that twinkle,
I'll iron out any wrinkle,
To keep your illness at bay

So we'll keep on pushing,
Making our way,
Down that winding road,
Carrying this heavy load,
Taking it day by day

III.

Love

Your Smile

Smiles provide rays of light
Like a one year old's first bite

Smiles deliver a certain flavor,
appeal
The kind you like to savor, feel

There's that smile that's says,
"Hey, I see you"
And in response, "Look who I'm married to!"

How about the smile that says,
"I had no clue until I met you."
Now I do

You got my number,
You dial my heart

True love from the start
I love your smile

✳

Rain Down On Me

When the rain falls
My heart stalls
Pain turns to joy,
Later withdrawals

Not just another day,
Hurt feelings gone astray
My love is back from holiday
Love is in season
You give me reason
To trust my heart,
Unconditionally

So you can rain down on me

I'll rain down on you
Dampen your pain,
Heartache with drizzle
From a four-alarm fire
Extinguished to a sizzle
Soak you with storms
As a cloud of love forms

Be my ocean.
My river.
My sea.
Won't you please
Rain down on me

✳

What To Do
With A Woman Like You

Every hour
Of every day,
Thoughts of you
Never far away
It's no surprise
With you time flies
What to do with a woman like you?

We get dressed up,
To go nowhere
You pretend
To be Rodgers,
Me Astaire
If you were a library book,
You'd forever be overdue,
What to do with a woman like you?

You bring me joy
Fill my heart with laughter
My before
My ever after
If you want to journey,
Together to the end

Yes, I do too!
What to do with a woman like you?

I will never make you blue
When I make love to you
It feels brand new

I know what to do with a woman like you.

＊

Better Days Ahead

Relax baby and chill
What we feel is real
You make my heart still.
You take my breath away

You may never know
How far I would go
Don't be misled
Better days ahead

We go together,
Like peanut butter and jam
Green eggs and ham
Butter on toasted bread
Better days ahead

My heart you'll mend
As my best friend
Up, up and away
Is where we'll stay

If I don't resist
You're what I've missed
This feels brand new
You erase all I've been through

You're my pain med
The remedy,
For better days ahead

We go together,
Like peanut butter and jam,
Green eggs and ham
Butter on toasted bread
Better days ahead

If you follow,
I'll swallow
My pride
Baby let's ride
You're first prize.

My love for you
I can not hide
Let your love unwind
You are my kind.

This coat of armor
You've helped me shed
You are the why
I no longer cry
Better days ahead

✳

Crazy, Love, Desire

Love is this and that,
Not magic you pull from a hat

You're an inspiration,
Penetrated my heart
I vote for till death do us part

You make me shake.
Rattle.
Roll to the core
Of my soul
In a way
I can't control

Temperature rising higher and higher
Can't deny the fire
A blaze
Crazy,
Love,
Desire

Once lost,
Now found
No more tears
Like that
Of a clown

You're a gift
No wrapping needed
Your love sincere
True without ego
Your devotion clear
I was grounded
Maybe never
to fly again.

I have rebounded,
You're a good friend

Once a
smoldering fire
Is now a raging
Crazy,
Love,
Desire

✳

IV.

Inspiration

In It To Win It

When shit hits the fan
You're doin' what you can
To the best of your ability
And still it's a stark reality

I'll keep my head up,
'Cause yup,
 Got to be,
Comin' back to me
Lady Luck

Love doesn't just show up,
Because you to say pick me
If you want it,
Go get it,
'Cause that's being,
In it to win it

Life's not always gonna be a blast
So be ready to kick some ass

We all fall
This we all have in common
Some come from a silver spoon
And live in a cocoon
Others laugh,
When they don't have,
Growing up eating Ramen

What is a trend,
Is where you start,
Is not where you end
Some folks stop and start,
Only to begin again
If you want it,
Go get it,
'Cause that's being,
In it to win it

*

Keep Believin'

Back in the day
There was no work,
Only play

A few bucks in my pocket
Along with a rocket
Life was a holiday

Ballin' in the park
Playin' until dark
Girls watching
And walking by
Got me jumping
So high

Today, things have a gone little awry

I never knew how many tears I held inside
At the drop of a hat,
A big cry

So many fears,
I can't lie
With the possibility,
B-Dub could die

Having Jazzy home,
Made dark times brighter
Escapade inspired,
I've become a
published writer

Wronged when
I was right.
Stayed strong,
Altered my plight

When things
happen for
no reason
Don't get down,
Get up,
Keep believin'

✳

After The Storm

Clouds can cast
Dark shadows and shades
I prefer greener pastures
Like the Everglades
Sometimes it's all spades

You can imagine,
But there is no truer discovery
Then to have the experience
Prevail

Misery loves company.
They'll try to tear you down.
With your character and presence
To no avail

They can not measure
The depth
Of what is inside of you,
Inside your heart.

And how you paved the way
For those you love
To have a better start

Thunder, lightening, and rain
Can cause a strain
While dark clouds shield the light,
Continue to form
Leaving much in tatters

There will always be bad weather.
That's the strife of life
It's what you do
After the storm
I'd say really matters

＊

Something Real

They say things happen for a reason
A sudden loss, you find yourself grieving
Affliction can lead to pill after pill
Addiction leads to self restriction
This is something real

You don't get to pick your family
Sometimes the closest is the enemy
When you're young and it happens,
You don't know what to feel,
Yet the pain is something real

You gave all of you to all of him,
In return he gifted you disparage
It's the sad truth,
You were a sleuth,
Ended the marriage
In the end, your spirit, he could not kill
What's inside you is something real

Lessons learned put you in check
Rack another deck,
Give me another deal
I'm a patient Mother'
Looking for something real

✳

The HandyMan Can

The real deal, I tell no lies
Big and black
A compromise
Gonna be me
For that
I don't apologize

A poodle dad,
Crushin' the stereotype
So Yo! no!
Don't believe the hype

Playing the game
Within the game
By the rules

Fueled by passion,
This HandyMan
Is utilizing his tools

The HandyMan can
'Cause he mixes it with love
And makes the world taste good
Like you know it should

✳

I Am

Feel the good vibration?
That's reality,
Not your imagination
Secure? Then no hesitation
Completed your intellectual migration
This is significant
You're not maleficent

What are you waiting for?
Fully charged, an online
You're ready to explore
A star ready to shine

You evened the score
You know how to grind

The pain you have endured
Is more than ample
Where you start
Is not where you end
You're the example

Belief in yourself is the core
For making the right choices

Volume down on the negativity,
Sky high are the positive voices

Life will go on
You'll again face adversity
That is a certainty

Find your center of gravity
Regain balance with levity

Won't settle, going for the slam
Here to stay, because I am

✳

Buried Treasure

Love what you see?
Good and plenty
This experience is not your history

You choose control
Over letting things be
Instead you'd rather rearrange me

Often we comply
Denying what is best
Caught up in emotions
Lingering notions
We acquiesce
I'll put this to rest
Get this off my chest
'Love me today,
And endlessly

Won't change to any degree
My core personality
Sound mind
Emotionally healthy

What you know,
Is what you know

Which didn't help you grow
In terms of relationships,
This is how you measure

I've passed go
Collected two hundo
We're like two passing ships
Won't be your buried treasure

*

Can You See Me

Where do you go
when you're tired of swiping
To and fro
But would like to be found

In your bubble with family, friends
On whom you depend
Wishing intimacy was around

You think you know goodness,
And an open heart
When you see it.
Yet judgment fails ya.

You give to receive
In the end you gift yourself a reprieve
A choice made that derails ya

You seem a broken record
Scratched and skipping
Like an LP
At the same place

This time seems different
It's the self reflection
And the footsteps you could retrace

Now look at your yard!
Though the times may have been hard,
Now you know the game
You're playing the right card

Your grounds are well manicured,
Shrubs groomed,
Flowers in bloom,
The grass green

No need to look
Your heart
An open book
You are seen

✳

V.

Introspective

Either Way

When do you decide
To allow something
To grow inside
Is it done with pride,
Or indecision?
Are you in agreement?
Or does it leave you
In division

Either way,
It's safe to say,
A child's life is at play

It's at this time we hear
merely our voices
Later they make
their own choices

Some in the big scope,
like dope, matter
Others create chatter,
And are great
Some think open

for debate
I think the latter

On your birthday
it's in your DNA,
Whether or not you
are straight or gay
Who cares anyway

What's important is
happiness on the inside
Life will provide
enough struggles of its own
The last thing they need
is for their parents not to condone

So forget what
you believe
Or what you've been taught
Into which you have bought

Just love them
for who they are
Roll down your sleeve
Be a shining star

✳

Red, White & Blue

So much going on
In our world today
Over here, over there

It was simpler back when they wondered
If the world was square

Later, cannons being fired,
The smell of gunpowder
Men are exhausted and tired
The enemy is drawing nearer
As shots ring louder

Presently we're clawing our way
Through a pandemic
Coping with variants
Trying to mime and mimic

We must stay on task
To continue lifting restraints,
Like wearing a mask

We do our best,
to celebrate
Those now at rest,
Who fought for America's
Self-interest

So tip your cap,
Remember those we came to in trust,
Who rose to the challenge for US

Fly vets fly way up
In the clear blue sky
And the heavens above

Your memories still shine bright.
Our freedom you preserved
We are one love

Happy Memorial Day

*

No Matter What The People Say

Relationships are hard enough,
If you're not on the same page,
It usually will fizzle out
Even with burning some sage

It's going along fine
Until one of you tries to rearrange
The thing that attracted you,
Is what you want to change?

You try to go about it
As if it remains the same
Tit for tat,
About this or that,
Now it's the blame game

When it comes to love making,
She's forsaking,
If she and her are not connected
If my insight is right, you will feel
No sex appeal
You'll get rejected

People are who they are
Up close or from afar

Groomed by yesterday,
Today, tomorrow,
And I don't know

Whether it's their hair,
Prayer, clothes,
Or they paint their toes
Expectance,
Allows the relationship
To like a river flow
Or a flower grow

Put your feet up.
Unwind.
Kick back
Pour a glass of wine.
From jump
She was my kind
We're doin' just fine

✳

With Kindness

Mmm..funny..
When you think about it
Even at birth
We start off as strangers

All of our emotions are learned responses
Some good, some bad,
Either way, we're re-arrangers

Parenting is not easy
Not like baking bread
Folding and kneading
As though children were dough

Consider fundamentals
Like never saying, "I told you so."
Guiding in place of lecturing
While they find their own way,
And grow

Remember to nurture them
Through those periods when they ask,
"Why that?" "Why this?"
It's just them being curious
At the end of the day,
I'd have to say,
My way,
Is with kindness

✳

Blue Days Gone

When the sunlight shines
Through the blinds
One looks, and quite often
Never finds
When your curtains are drawn,
Hope has dissipated or gone

To compensate for a decision,
Cutting an incision,
Culminating into a mistake

A better choice may be to doodle,
Play poodle
And enjoy the break

For some, time alone is a challenge,
Challenging to condone

We should all try spending time
In solitary
No tv, computer, phone

Feelings can be responsible
For the many directions in which we're lured

You may never be cured
Get your house in order,
Your lawn manicured
Only then is a quality relationship assured

Until then, take care of you
Those in your crew
Green is better than blue
Many friends come down to a few

✳

This Little Birdie

Long and arduous road
Under duress
Bearing quite the load

The community
Stood behind me
Never alone
Outpouring of love
By letter and phone

Those who saw me opposite the glass
Believed in my future because of my past

We tried circumventing the court
Thwarted by the DA's report

Unable to see
The one I love most
She held it down,
In the background,
She's the JazzBerry
On my buttered toast

Going home
Awarded probation
Back to BBX
My baby
My creation

Time to move on
Put past behind us
In me I trust
I write
To right
A wrong
A sad song

Turned a bust
An unjust
Into a plus

Craving fresh air
And a Coca-Cola
Me and my girl
Headed to Capitola

Finally a release date,
After much debate,
McClinton v the State
Six months too late
To cross home plate,
Left me irate
Much to contemplate

In the end,
My heart found love
Buried the anger and hate

This little birdie is in route
Leaving behind the orange suit

*

Photosynthesis

Plant seeds, flowers will grow
Environment dictates quality
Sometimes you don't know

Watering, light, pruning,
You'll see green,
And colors bright

Without these essentials,
Realistically,
Life ends one
day or night

Pick your parents
Change your path
Alter your plight

We can't
Don't rave and rant
Pick up the pieces
Write a thesis
Darkness can be light

Sounds strange?
So does change!
Never too late,
Stay true
The rest will come

Not the start,
That defines how smart
It's the whole
Not the parts
That total the sum

✳

The Real Deal

You're smart
Didn't have to study hard
You can memorize
Great recall

To start,
Be vulnerable,
Drop your guard
You'll realize,
You didn't learn at all

Reality can be stark
Third times the charm
At what cost?
No substitute for experience

You missed the mark
Gotta twist your arm
Look what you've lost
Because of your insistence

Lesson well learned
Opportunity not wasted
Not the worst you've tasted
Yet still not a good feel
Wounds can scar,
They will heal

Recovery hurts,
If earned
Remember when your heart got burned?
You wouldn't if you could
So goes life

That's the real deal

✳

VI.

The Pandemic

Are You Ready?

Wow...
Sometimes I wonder
How I've managed
The last year and a half
To maintain empathy
Much coming at me
Still found humor
And a way to laugh

Schools decided online was best
For students and faculty's interest

This wasn't good
Jazzy made the best,
From bad that she could

It was so easy,
Been this way for so long
It's a revelation
We've had three altercations
The third,
Admittedly, I was wrong

Nine months together
I will cherish forever

The highlight alone
At number one,
Never to be outdone,
We watched Hamliton

Not only did we wine, dine
And fill our belly
I got even closer,
To big Sis Nellie

Met every Friday night,
Each a sweet delight,
A real thriller
Cooked, cried, talked, vibed
We were each other's pillar

When the struggle is real,
And it's pain you feel,
Don't run from it
Run to it

Find a way to deal
Stand strong,
Like Valyrian Steel

You never know,
When the earth may quake
Things begin to shake
Making footing unsteady

Ask yourself,
When the likes,
Of disaster strikes,

Are you ready?

✳

The Mask

You can't see,
What's behind the mask
Is a mystery
The eyes,
A window of such,
Tells much
Otherwise a mere disguise

In comes the fashion,
Choices of style
Out goes the hello
Leaving a displaced smile

The mask affords you protection
From contracting the infection
Not like a rubber mask,
You might need
In the event of an erection

As the mask fades away
No more under cover
You're on full display

In the end,
Duty and purpose was served,
Completed its task
A super hero of sorts,
With no cape
Known simply as,
The Mask

*

With Love

Life happens,
You move forward
With decisions you've made
Leaving behind experiences
In lieu of memories
That never fade

Molded by the environment in which we live
We learn to either take or find more love to give
Nature or nurture, I'm not sure which one got the part
The role defined sympathy and empathy of the heart

We need to heed this more now than ever before
Instead we stand, closed hand, ready to fight, while I write

I write to keep my heart open, hoping for positive change
Unemployment on the rise, Covid demise, times are strange

We need kindness to remind us of the importance of love
Whether you believe in karma, spirituality or the man above
Hate we cannot tolerate, we must conquer ignorance with love

*

As The Pandemic Turns

Be grateful,
During these times,
If you're lucky enough to have a job
Some turn to vodka, gin, rum
Others choose to scam, scheme, and rob

The marriage had issues
On cruise control
Cheating with a lover pre-pandemic

Now you see what your marriage lacks,
The disfunction is systemic

For Christ sake,
Caught a damn break
Unemployment pays more than you make

You're single
You can't mix, mingle
Online chatting,
Perhaps you Zoom

No face to face
That's the wrong song
In your dorm,
Alone in your room

Can you relate?
To one or all of the above
What's needed is empathy and love

Take a moment to reflect
I suspect,
You'll uncover,
Rediscover,
While you noodle

To handle this strife in life,
Perhaps you need a Standard Poodle?

✳

VII.

Injustice

Eyes Wide Open

You ever want to disappear, or be invisible
Depressed, anxious, afraid, miserable.

Well, what if it was something even sadder
Something so entrenched in our fabric
Like Black Lives Matter

You roll down the street
For a bite to eat
Next thing you know,
Okay, now here we go
To your demise and frustration
Next thing you hear is
"License and registration."

What seems like a simple traffic stop
Turns into, pop, pop, pop,
A tombstone, with your name on top

I live with this fear everyday
Tell my daughter she'll be okay
So when you wish upon a star
Remember these words from FDR
"Nothing to fear but Fear Itself."

Sure, when racism is on the shelf

✳

The Verdict

Racism, police brutality
Reality
In America

Shouldn't be,
Unfortunately,
In our fabric it's woven
Laid out by Derick Shauvin

Found guilty
By a jury
Justice served,
Instead of pity

"Blue Wall" an institution
This time retribution
Yet one verdict is not the solution
Police station's still full of pollution

No longer disbelief
The verdict a relief
From sadness and grief

✳

VIII.

Loss

Elements & Despair

So much angst, anxiety, despair
Over here, over there
Fires raging in the west,
destroying homes, lives,
Leaving behind smoked filled air

A challenge to lace them up, go to work
Burying thoughts and worries
Trying not to contemplate
As if Covid was not enough,
forced to evacuate
A category four hurricane,
Sixteen years to the date

Prayers, thoughts, positive vibes,
food rations, donations
Go out to so many
I reflect
using my intellect
on my deck,
surrounded by two white Standards
and a black Mini

✳

The Strife Of Life

How do we handle someone leaving?
We all go through grieving

A hamster
A dog
A cat
As a child
May the first,
Be like that

Prime years no fears,
Of loss near and dear
What we believe,
May not yet be clear.

It seems
In just days
Another friend
has cancer
Some survive.
Recover.
Thrive

Others have therapy
Fight to get healthy
Then finally,
There's no answer

High School aggravation
College graduation
Wedding invitation
Flowers and trips,
To our parents grave

Prosperity
and success
we gain,
Can't save us
From heartache, pain

Don't know if we come back
For another lap around the track

Won't waste a day,
Living a hurtful way

✳

Rest In Peace

Life has a flow,
A kind of rhythm.
A delicate balancing act

Life can be temperamental,
Even inconsequential,
Lead you down the wrong track

When things do go awry,
One should ask why
They come to another conclusion.

A false sense of security,
Unhealthy,
A lapse of maturity
Making life an illusion

There are many pathways
Leading to such a dark place of affliction

The road to hell,
Mapped out in detail,
Known to derail
Is addiction

So Rest In Peace my short time friend
Sadly it's come to and end

Your life shouldn't have ended like this
Your passion and your smile
 I'll forever miss

*

VIII.

Friendship

Stay Awhile

Much is expressed
Through touch, embrace
Communication key,
Love grew, with pace
And space

You know those times,
When few words
Need to be spoken
Your rhythm
My rhymes,
Our hearts,
Our minds,
Our intimacy,
Got me chokin'

How often do we listen,
While preparing to respond,
Without hearing?

If this is your approach,
You'll receive reproach,
For not being endearing

The heart may be
On foot patrol,
The eyes remain
The windows to the soul

You can run,
You can't hide,
What's inside
Heartache. Pain.
Take their toll

The eyes don't lie
No matter how hard you try
Sadness is not your style

If you cry, or you're feeling blue,
Your face can't deny
So sit
Stay a while.

✳

My Nubian Queen

I imagine her skin, like satin
A pretty dark brown
Curves, swerves, and junk
In the trunk to go around

A rock on which I can lean
She's the real thing
My Nubian Queen

Much attitude,
not to be confused,
With rude
She's my bestie
My Big Lebowski
She's my Dude

As important as she is to me
The equivalent to her
Her family
They opened their hearts
Accepted me
Now an extended branch of their genealogy

Inside out she's pristine
Together we've cried
My Nubian Queen

Forever and a day,
Won't be long enough
That final goodbye
Is going to be rough

Between now and later,
There's nothing greater,
Than a Friday night delight,
Sharing the scene,
With my Nubian Queen

✳

That Time Of Year

The inevitable
time of year
We celebrate
with holiday cheer
Sounds good
to the average ear
Not so much,
If you don't have
someone near
And dear

Singular in terms
Of holidays commercialized
Took a minute,
But now I've realized,
Much to my
Chagrin and threatened demise

Doesn't matter
The gift or the size
It's the ones who can't give,
More than the ones that can
Who cries
About the tears in
their children's eyes

It should mean more
Than who does,
Or doesn't come
Through that door

Perhaps there's
some family issue
Or some unsettled score

If we judged less,
Converted prejudice,
Of any kind,
Into interest,
We'd be well blessed

With this I'll end
Please share with a friend

Hopes and prayers go out to those who have less

Find a way to still manage to have a Merry Christmas

✳

IX.

Pain

It's Only Rain

Sky darkens
Gonna storm
Batten the hatches
Comin' in batches
It's only rain

You mean so
much to me
The whole
world can see
You flood my heart
It's only rain

Barometric pressure falls
Ring around the moon
Feels like a monsoon
It's only rain

Cirrus clouds fly by
Goodbye blue sky
Hail can be hell
It's only rain

✳

Why Can't I Say Goodbye?

We were rolling,
Rolling a long
Harmonious in song

Minds melding
together
Bodies welding
forever
So I thought,
When abruptly it
all went wrong

I can't breathe

How could we be through
I will never get over you

You were my drug.
Your love kept me so high
I'm addicted to you
I can't quit
I need another hit
Why can't I say goodbye?

You were my all in one
So much variety
I thought the withdrawals were done
No. The pain is the same,
Along with anxiety

I can't breathe.

If it's the same old,
How can I ever start anew?
It feels like it was all a lie
All I do is think of you and cry
Why can't I say goodbye?

You knew my body in every way
Never a word did I have to say
My lust for you on full display
She was your dessert,
After the entree

I can't breathe

The hurt, a deep ache.
Can you for sake?
I let out a Yelp
To feel you one more time,
Would be so sublime
I know it won't help

I can't breathe

I'm all cried out
I feel like I'm going to die
Why can't I say goodbye?

*

On The Outside Looking In

Touching, feeling,
Deeply impacts the senses
Not ready?
There are consequences

We're not meant to be alone
I've made mistakes, which I own

You were right
I was wrong
It's you,
For whom I long
This is my song

What we had was ecstasy
I was blind
Now I see my reality
You spoke,
Broke
Away from me

It's my fault.
I got caught
Now I'm lonely
I apologize for all the lies

Respectfully,
Please here my plea

Is there a way
To make it ok?
Go back,
Start all over again?
I don't want to be,
Hopelessly,
Forever in sin
On the outside looking in

∗

Wrong Time, Right Place

Inundated with you're the one
I hesitated, started to run

With you pulsing through my veins,
These were different kind of chest pains

It all happened so fast
I wanted it to last
Now it's long ago
And hardly a hello

Occasional spat,
About this or that
Never enough time
Flowed like a rhyme

We felt it deep
Glad for what we had
Our challenge was steep

As sure as after day, night will fall
I believe we could have had it all

Any wrong we made right
Making love later that night

Taught me to explore
To be open to more

Most will never know
Most will put on a show
Most don't know how to share
No other love will ever compare

I'll always love what we had
The void that makes me sad

Still today
I feel the same way
You're the gift
The reason I'm okay

Any wrong we made right
Making love later that night

Taught me to explore
To be open to more

With you lust became a reality
My insecurities, the real enemy
Taught me how to love

And it started with me

I was too young to know
A seed buried waiting to grow
You helped me find my shine
My inner glow

There are times your footsteps,
You can retrace
For us there will never be
That time or place

*

X.

The Struggle

Story of My Heart

I have to begin at the end
When I married a friend
This is where I start,
To tell the story of my heart

No more peace
Declared war
Wounded, bleeding
Fed some of what I wanted
Mostly starved
Hungry for what I was needing

I wouldn't understand what it means to be a man
Without struggle, heartache and pain
To teach me I can

Jail was hell
Held without bail
Six months in solitary
It's about the mail
Built my own library
No matter what caper
Printed in the newspaper
No Internet, ousted from the grid
Trying to wear me down

Nope. My mind is sound
Both feet on solid ground
No reboot, for I had heart
From the very start.
I don't harbor hate
Or discriminate.
Be vulnerable, empathetic, that's what I believe
Heart ring and necklace, the one on my sleeve

Love is my thing
Passion I bring
Joy that makes the soul sing
Money buys you bling,
But not one good friend
Which in the end
Is everything

Though I did not finish college
I possess an unquenchable thirst
For knowledge
Some I have shared and cared to impart
Outlining, defining the story of my heart.

✷

Reflection

The night rolls along
Along with song
It feels wrong
My heart knows it's right

It's okay to feel lonely,
There are many
You're not the one and only
It matters, but not really

Comfortable alone, I believe you must be
If not, commitment, at best, is risky

It starts with a road we've yet to travel
It's no mystery, without a foundation,
How quickly it unravels

At that point,
It's a coin flip,
That determines a good or bad trip

Education laggin'
Don't end up in the paddy wagon
Wearing an orange suit,
Crocks, and pants saggin'

If you want better opportunities
Than some in your family tree,
You must strive to survive,
Focus, prioritize, and want to be....

A better dad, than I had
A faithful husband with kids who are healthy
Understand that money alone won't make you wealthy

Find the truth in you.
When you do
Share it
But never let go

When you do,
I assure you,
Your heart will shine
Those around you will grow
Like berries on a vine
It'll get sweeter with time

✳

Breaker Of Chains

Some are fortunate enough
To attend a school titled Day
Others aren't so lucky,
They just pretend
Make their way

If one gets across the tracks
Overcoming what he or she lacks,
Stay focused.
You look forward
But always remember the givebacks

That day when you do arrive,
Inside you had that drive,
To reach high and strive

It's bigger than you,
You accomplished a lot
For being a have-not,
Yet there's more to do

Turned a dirt road into a lane
Suffered so to ease their pain
Displayed discipline
What others cited mundane
You completed the cycle.
You have broken the chain

Me & My 3

My growing up lay far from normal
Most lessons I learned
I'd categorize informal

It's the opening, not the end game

I listened,
So again not be christened
Upside the head.
Surrounded by so many addictions
Accompanied with just as many restrictions

It's the opening, not the end game

The best gift ever given
Is probably why I'm still livin'
The opportunity to move to Cali
Gave me the chance to rally

It's the opening, not the end game

With my heart and my soul,
My only goal
To pave the way for my JazzBerry
I'd say she's on a roll,

An old soul.
Now she's playing soccer
At a New England school

It's the opening, not the end game

Now, I'm geared up for the second half
For a partner with whom I can laugh

It's the opening, not the end game

At this point the last page must remain
At this point, we have to see the same
End game

Otherwise, it will be happily
Me and my 3

Make Rain Fall

Sometimes you take a chance
It's worth it to go the distance
With the wind at your back,
Rolling like thunder, no resistance

When you arrive,
Will it be what you hoped it would be?
If you don't go,
You won't know
 It'll be a mystery

If we all had a crystal ball,
It would be easy to make that call
We don't, and won't

When you get there, be there
Make rainfall

Right or wrong,
We're not here long
No time to waste
Most like vanilla,
I find dark chocolate
Is an acquired taste

Life has you in stitches
Could bring you riches,
Could bring handsome, dark, tall
Or nothing at all

Happiness is not a given,
You're busy dying or livin'
Treat every day as,
If it were your last call.
Make rain fall

✳

Abstract

A Door Is Not Just A Door

They come in different dimensions, shapes
Like trap doors, often used for escapes
A door, for sure, is not just the door

A door is not just an opening,
Horizontal with the floor
It's an opening or a gateway
To something new to explore

A door can open, close on its own
Unlike a broken heart
Or one bursting apart
Neither one happens alone

Then there's your car door
If it's Porsche,
It's like sitting on the floor
Surrounded by superficial rapport
At least you have speed galore

If you're thirsty,
And Kirsty
Doesn't quench your thirst,
You'll want more
Give this some thought first

Better to walk out the door,
Before the same woman
That made you feel loved and adorned,
Realizes it's you she despises
Now a woman scorned

You saw the stop signs,
Which you chose to ignore
Now you're off track
Like a broken garage door

Check yourself,
Before you wreck yourself
You know this relationship
will not endure

Folks bag their skeletons,
Hide secrets behind closet doors
But once revealed,
Your fate is sealed
Truth exudes your pores

A door is not just a door
Many types for sure
Hopefully after reading this,
You'll think of doors
Differently than you did before

✳

Traffic Lights Up My Life

I wouldn't say I'm lazy,
Though I enjoy hanging out

I like photography
I capture moments
That erase any doubt

My favorite colors,
As long as I can remember,
Are red, yellow and green

People are funny,
If I don't flash these colors,
I create quite the scene

I've always been the quiet type,
There you stand with poise,
Until I make some noise

It is not all glitz and glamor,
This point I am going to hammer,
It gets lonely night after night

The air has a bit of chill
I'm swinging a bit, but mostly still
I would kill
To signal left or right

This is my life
I didn't choose it
So I didn't have a chance,
To lose it
I'm going to hang in here
Do my thing

I look on the bright side,
As I think, "That's a nice ride!"
You could be,
Hopelessly, lying around,
Waiting for someone to ring

*

I'm Not My Hair

Blond, brunette, red head, maybe dark brown
Hair's just a noun
I'd cut it down
It's much work to wear the crown

Colored, textured, spiked, layered
Samson I'm not,
I've never cared
Those closest are very much the crutch
Want to be better now?

Don't wait for later
Be a creator
Look into the mirror
Wake up

Somehow
When there is no more there there,
You realize it's just hair

I'm not my hair
Au contraire

*

XII.

Hope

A Brighter Day

Away with sorrow
On with tomorrow
If there's a will,
There's a way
Sunset gives birth
To a brighter day.

✳

CPSIA information can be obtained
at www.ICGtesting.com
Printed in the USA
BVHW061937220522
637756BV00014B/181

9 780990 683117